Bible-based activities to strengthen Christian values

The buyer of this book may reproduce pages for classroom or home use. Duplication for any other use is prohibited without written permission from David C. Cook Publishing Co.

Copyright ©1994 David C. Cook Publishing Co. Printed in the United States of America.

All puzzles and Bible activities are based on the NIV.

Scripture taken from the Holy Bible, New International Version, Copyright ©1973, 1978, 1984 International Bible Society. Used by permission of Zondervan Bible Publishers.

ISBN: 0-7814-5091-8

Edited by Debbie Bible
Book Design by Jack Rogers
Cover Illustration by Corbin Hillam
Interior Illustrations by Barbara Todd & Corbin Hillam

TABLE OF CONTENTS

Introduction for Adult Friends of Children 3-4
What Is Being Responsible? 5
The Bible Tells about Being Responsible
    Caleb Follows Through 6-7
Caleb Shows He Was Responsible 8
Being Responsible Takes Practice 9
A Puzzle about Being Responsible 10
Responsible for Yourself 11
Changing Your Words 12
Actions with Hands and Feet 13
Doing Your Part—Galatians 6:4 14
Doing the Responsible Thing 15
Children and Right Actions 16
Reminding Yourself 17
A Responsibility Clock 18
The Bible Tells about Being Responsible
    Paul Continues the Work He Started 19-20
Talking with Actions 21
Responsible Acrostic 22
The Value of Being Responsible 23

What is Being Merciful? 24
The Bible Tells about Being Merciful
    Abigail Helps David Show Mercy 25-26
Puppets for a Play about Mercy 27-28
Abigail and David Show Mercy
    A Puppet Play based on 1 Samuel 25:2-35 29-30
150-Year-Old Code 31
Merciful Bookmark 32
What is Mercy? 33
Show Mercy to All People 34
Words about Being Merciful 35
The Bible Tells about Being Merciful
    Jesus Tells a Story 36-37
A Game about Mercy 38-39
Loving Mercy - Micah 6:8 40
Where Should I Show Mercy? 41
The Value of Being Merciful 42
Value Builders Series Index 43-48

RESPONSIBLE & MERCIFUL

INTRODUCTION FOR ADULT FRIENDS OF CHILDREN
(Parents, Teachers, and Other Friends of Children)

Values. What are they? How do we acquire them? Can we change them?

"Values" is a popular term, usually meaning *the standard that governs how one acts and conducts one's life.* Our personal standards, or values, are learned and adapted, possibly changed and relearned, over a lifetime of experiences and influences.

Children begin acquiring personal values at birth. As parents, teachers, and other adults who love children, we are concerned that they are learning worthwhile values, rather than being randomly influenced by everything around them. By God's design, we cannot control the process of acquiring values, but we can influence the process in a variety of ways. Our consistent modeling of biblical values is a vital influence, but children must also be encouraged to talk about specific values and be aware of these values in action in themselves and others.

These biblical values are God's values. He has established His standards to help us know how to live our lives and how we are to treat other people. Our goal is to have these biblical values be a part of each child's experience.

A value becomes one's own when a person chooses to act on that value consistently. Saying that we hold to the value of honesty, yet bending the truth or telling a lie when pressured is a contradiction.

Providing opportunities for children to investigate a specific value, identifying with people in the Bible who have that value, and trying to put it into practice in real life situations will help strengthen the value in the lives of the children and reinforce its importance. The purpose of the Value Builders Series is to provide such opportunities.

This book in the Value Builders Series focuses on **being responsible** and **being merciful**. Being responsible is defined as *being someone who can be depended on to do both what needs to be done and the things you say you'll do.* Caleb and Paul are two biblical examples of responsible people. They showed us how they took responsibility for themselves as well as for the tasks God had asked them to do.

Being merciful is *treating someone kindly instead of giving punishment, even when punishment is deserved.* God showed us mercy by providing His Son as our means of personal salvation. We are to be merciful to each other, forgiving the hurts we receive, rather than giving out punishment.

Abigail helps David decide to be merciful instead of giving punishment to Nabal. Jesus' story about the servant who receives mercy but is unwilling to give it

RESPONSIBLE & MERCIFUL

is another example for us from the Bible.

The Value Builders Series provides Bible story activities, craft activities, and life application activities that focus on specific biblical values. These books can be used by children working alone, or the pages can be reproduced and used in a classroom setting.

In a classroom setting, this book could be used to supplement curriculum that you are using, or it can be used as a curriculum itself in a 30-55 minute period. Each page is coded at the bottom to suggest where it might fit in a teaching session. The codes are as follows:

🔓 = Definition page

📖 = Bible Story page

 = Craft page

 = Life Application page

Some suggestions for using the materials in this book in a 30-55 minute period are:

5-10 minutes:	Introduce the value and discuss the definition. Use pages entitled, "What Is Being Responsible?" or "What Is Being Merciful?"
10-15 minutes:	Present one of the Bible stories using appropriate pages. Encourage the children to describe what it might have been like to be in that situation and what other things could have happened.
10-20 minutes:	Choose life application activity pages or craft activities that are appropriate to the children in your class. Design some group applications for the pages you have chosen.
5-10 minutes:	To conclude, use the page entitled, "The Value of Being Responsible," or "The Value of Being Merciful" and encourage the children to make a commitment to focus on this value for the next few days or weeks. Pray for God's help to guide the children as they learn to live by His standards.

...b Follows Through

(...-24 continued from page 6)

...gone up with him [Caleb] ... spread among the Israelites a ... d they had explored. ...

...people ... grumbled against Moses and Aaron and the whole ... them, " ... Why is the Lord bringing us to this land only to let us ...d? ...."

...es and Aaron ... Joshua ... and Caleb ... entire Israelite assembly, "The land we passed ...and explored is exceedingly good. If the Lord is ... with us, he will lead us into that land, ... and ...ve it to us. Only do not rebel against the Lord. ... ...ord is with us. Do not be afraid of them."

"EXCEEDINGLY GOOD" MEANS IT WAS VERY, VERY, VERY GOOD. LIKE GRAPE JELLY MADE FROM THOSE GIANT GRAPES!

But the whole assembly talked about stoning them. Then the glory of the Lord appeared at the Tent of Meeting to all the Israelites. The Lord said to Moses, "How long will these people treat me with contempt? How long will they refuse to believe in me, in spite of all the miraculous signs I have performed among them? ...."

Moses said to the Lord, " ... In accordance with your great love, forgive the sin of these people. ...."

The Lord replied, "I have forgiven them, as you asked. Nevertheless, ... No one who has treated me with contempt will ever see it. But because my servant Caleb has a different spirit and follows me wholeheartedly, I will bring him into the land he went to, and his descendants will inherit it."

✎ **Put the names of the twelve explorers in alphabetical order. Start with Ammiel. Then circle the names of the two men who said, "It is a good land. God has promised to help us. We should move there."**

Shammua	1. Ammiel
Shaphat	2.
Caleb	3.
Igal	4.
Joshua	5.
Palti	6.
Gaddiel	7.
Gaddi	8.
Ammiel	9.
Sethur	10.
Nahbi	11.
Geuel	12. Shaphat

VALUE BUILDERS
RESPONSIBLE & MERCIFUL

✏️ **Fix the spacing in these words.** The firs...

Caleb showed he was being RESPONSIBLE when he . . .

1. fol lowed/Mos es'instr ucti ons. Mos essai dtolo okover the... someof th efr uit.

2. beli evedGo dwoul ddow hatHes aidHew oulddo. Gods aidth atHe... givethem th eland.

3. hel pedMo sest otel lth epeo pletha tGo dwou ldhe lpth em.

✏️ **Write the name of the person who did each action. If no one di... cross out the statement.**

Caleb   the other explorers   Moses

1. _____ knew he was responsible for himself and to God for his own actions.

2. _____ followed Moses' instructions to go and explore the new land.

3. _____ changed his mind and came home after five days.

4. _____ believed that God would do what He said He would.

5. _____ thought that God couldn't protect them in the new land.

6. _____ obeyed God by telling the people that God would help them go to the new land.

7. _____ told Moses he wouldn't go to explore the new land.

RESPONSIBLE FOR YOURSELF

Just like Galatians 6:4 says, take pride in yourself and carry your own load!

What are you responsible for? ✏ **Write on each line what you are responsible for.**

MYSELF
Brushing teeth
Knowing God
_____
_____
_____

MY HOME
Cleaning my room
_____
_____
_____
_____

MY FAMILY
Sharing my love
_____
_____
_____
_____

MY FRIENDS
Homework help
_____
_____
_____
_____

MY NEIGHBORHOOD
Helping at church
_____
_____
_____
_____

CHANGING YOUR WORDS

What about the times you only want to do something because you know you will get a reward? The responsible thing is to do something because it is the RIGHT thing to do, not necessarily to get something back in return. ✎ **Change each of these responses below to be responsible ones.**

ACTIONS WITH HANDS AND FEET

Mouths, hands, and feet help us to be responsible. If you say (with your mouth) that you are going to do something, then be sure to follow through (with your hands and feet.) **Draw a line to match these hands and feet.**

DOING YOUR PART— GALATIANS 6:4

Galatians 6:4 tells us about being responsible. **Find the matching puzzle pieces and write the correct word in each piece to complete the verse.**
HINT: Some words are used more than once.

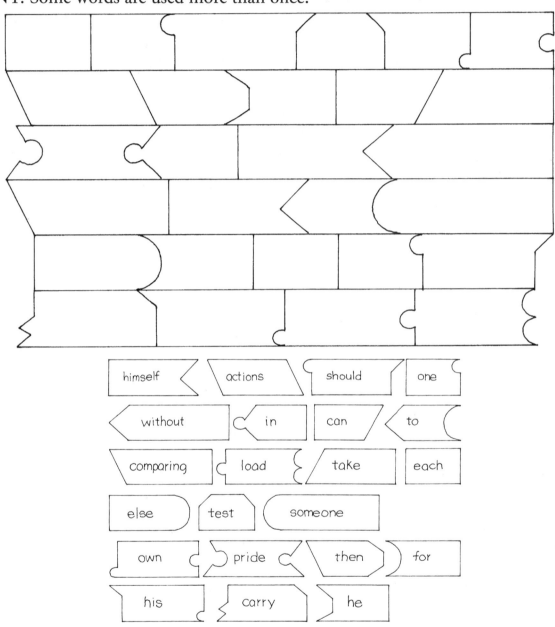

✎ **Write YES before each true statement about yourself.**

____ I do what I say I will do. (My actions are the test. I get an A!)
____ I take responsibility for the things I should. (I carry my own load.)
____ I don't compare myself with others. My responsibilities are different from theirs.
____ I am proud of myself for doing the right thing, even if other kids don't do it.

DOING THE RESPONSIBLE THING

What do you think? ✎ **Write your response to each situation.**

You already have a lot of homework and now the teacher assigns a new project, due next week. There is a Sunday school class party on Saturday and church on Sunday. It doesn't look like you have enough time to do everything. What is a responsible thing to do?

_____
_____

You are babysitting for two little children. Right after the parents leave the dog gets sick on the kitchen floor. You didn't <u>say</u> you would take care of the dog, but the parents won't be home for several hours. And you really <u>don't</u> want to clean up after the dog! What is a responsible thing to do?

_____
_____

Your dad told everyone in the family about saving the chips, popcorn, and soda for Friday night. But it's Wednesday afternoon, you are s-t-a-r-v-i-n-g, and dinner isn't for two more hours. Since no one else is home, you're thinking of eating just a few chips and drinking a soda. What is a responsible thing to do?

_____
_____

You just tore the screen on the back door when you rushed outside. Even though it's summer and the door stays open a lot, you don't think anyone will notice the tear. So you're not sure if you should say anything or not. What is a responsible thing to do?

_____
_____

CHILDREN AND RIGHT ACTIONS

✎ **Fill in the underlined words in the puzzle.**

Proverbs 20:11

Even a <u>child</u> is <u>known</u> by his <u>actions</u>, by <u>whether</u> his <u>conduct</u> is <u>pure</u> and <u>right</u>.

✎ **Now, write this verse in your own words.**

_____
_____
_____
_____
_____

"CONDUCT" AND "ACTIONS" ARE TWO WAYS TO SAY THE SAME THING.

16

REMINDING YOURSELF

"Jordan, the laundry is still sitting here waiting for you to fold it. You agreed that this was the job you wanted as your part of our family responsibilities."

What can Jordan do to remind HIMSELF about his folding responsibility?

What would you do if you needed to remind YOURSELF about something you said you would do?

One good thing about being a frog is no laundry to fold. Then maybe we could help Jordan do his. Being responsible is seeing what needs to be done and doing it.

✏️ **Choose one of these ways and then DO the way you choose.**

A.
- Set an alarm clock to go off at the time you need to do what you said.
- Put the clock in a place you can easily see it.
- Set the clock every day you need to remind yourself about something.

B.
- Make a clock like the one on page 18.
- Hang the clock in your room where you can see it often.

C.
- Make a chart on a large sheet of paper.
- Write the days of the week across the top.
- List the things to do on the left side.
- Put a check mark when you have done something.

D. Can you come up with another idea?
_____
_____
_____
_____

A RESPONSIBILITY CLOCK

Learning to be responsible includes reminding yourself about what you need to do. ✏️ **Create a clock that can be set at the time you need to do something. Make this clock as unusual as possible so you will enjoy looking at it everyday.**

You need:
- ☐ Colored poster board
- ☐ Ruler
- ☐ Paper fastener
- ☐ Scissors
- ☐ Markers
- ☐ Twelve or more 3" x 5" cards
- ☐ Glue
- ☐ Magazine pictures of faces of all age people

✂️ **To make a Responsibility Clock:**
1. Cut an 8" x 28" piece of poster board.
2. Draw a line 8" from one end and use that 8" square to draw a clock face.
3. Make two poster board hands for the clock one 4" x 3/4", the other 3" x 3/4". Attach these to the middle of the clock face with the paper fastener.
4. Fold a 3" x 5" card in half to make a 5" long fold as a Responsibility Card Holder. Glue one side of this card to the clock about three inches below the clock face with the fold side down to create a "V".
5. Decorate the area below the clock face using the magazine pictures of faces. Create a collage by overlapping the edges of the pictures and covering the entire 8" x 20" with faces.

✂️ **To make Responsibility Cards:**
1. Use a 3" x 5" card to write something you need to remind yourself about.
2. Set the hands on the clock to the time you need to do what is written on the card.
3. Put the card on the holder below the time set.

LET'S MAKE A RESPONSIBILITY CLOCK AND DECORATE IT WITH FROG FACES!

GOOD IDEA! LET'S HOP TO IT!

THE BIBLE TELLS ABOUT BEING RESPONSIBLE

Paul Continues the Work He Started

Acts 9:15; 20:2-38

But the Lord said [about Paul], "This man is my chosen instrument to carry my name before the Gentiles and their kings and before the people of Israel."

[Paul] traveled through that area, speaking many words of encouragement to the people, and finally arrived in Greece, . . .

From Miletus, Paul sent to Ephesus for the elders of the church. When they arrived, he said to them: "You know how I lived the whole time I was with you, . . . that I have not hesitated to preach anything that would be helpful to you but have taught you publicly and from house to house. I have declared to both Jews and Greeks that they must turn to God in repentance and have faith in our Lord Jesus.

"And now, compelled by the Spirit, I am going to Jerusalem not knowing what will happen to me there. I only know that in every city the Holy Spirit warns me that prison and hardships are facing me. However, I consider my life worth nothing to me, if only I may finish the race and complete the task the Lord Jesus has given me—the task of testifying to the gospel of God's grace.

(Read the rest of the story on page 20)

"TESTIFYING" MEANS HE WAS TELLING EVERYONE!

✏️ **Find these phrases in the Bible story and underline them. Draw a line to the sentence that defines each one.**

1. chosen instrument — The Lord asked Paul to explain who Jesus is and how people can know Him.

2. carry my name — Paul was going to Jerusalem because He knew that was what God wanted him to do.

3. compelled by the Spirit — Paul was picked by God to travel around telling people about Jesus.

4. my life worth nothing, if only — The most important thing in Paul's life was to follow God's plan for his life rather than his own.

THE BIBLE TELLS ABOUT BEING RESPONSIBLE

Paul Continues the Work He Started

(Acts 9:15; 20:2-38 continued from page 19)

"Now I know that none of you among whom I have gone about preaching the kingdom will ever see me again. . . .

"Now I commit you to God. . . . I have not coveted anyone's silver or gold or clothing. You yourselves know that these hands of mine have supplied my own needs and the needs of my companions. In everything I did, I showed you that by this kind of hard work we must help the weak, remembering the words the Lord Jesus himself said: 'It is more blessed to give than to receive.'"

"COVETED" MEANS HE WANTED FOR HIMSELF WHAT BELONGED TO ANOTHER PERSON.

When he had said this, he knelt down with all of them and prayed. They all wept as they embraced him and kissed him. What grieved them most was his statement that they would never see his face again. Then they accompanied him to the ship.

✏️ **Read the following statements about Paul. If a statement tells something responsible that Paul did, draw this symbol ⓡ on the blank. If a statement is not something a responsible person would do, draw this symbol ⓡ̸ on the blank.**

1. _____ preached things that were helpful to the people.

2. _____ followed Jesus' instructions to him about preaching how people should repent and believe on Jesus.

3. _____ told Jesus he would preach and then didn't do it.

4. _____ took care of his own needs for money and clothing.

5. _____ didn't help anyone even though he knew how to help.

6. _____ wanted someone else to take care of his food and clothes.

7. _____ worked hard to help those who needed it.

8. _____ didn't bother to tell people about Jesus.

TALKING WITH ACTIONS

Proverbs 20:11 says "Even a child is known by his actions, by whether his conduct is pure and right." People can tell whether you are a responsible person or not by what you do. ✎ **Complete the sentences by changing each letter to the letter that comes before it in the alphabet.**

Your actions and your conduct are

uif uijoht zpv ep _____

uif xbz zpv bdu _____

uif uijoht zpv tbz _____

Your actions are pure and right when you

ep uif uijoht hpe ufbdift jo uif cjcmf

_____

pcfz zpvs qbsfout boe ufbdifst

_____

ep xibu zpv tbz zpv xjmm ep

_____

bsf sftqpotjcmf gps xibu zpv ep

_____

✎ **Draw a picture of yourself in the act of being responsible.**

If you want to see action, I'll show you some very active actions! Watch me hop 500 meters!

You have an active imagination, too. That was more like a 5-inch hop.

The active part is right, anyway.

RESPONSIBLE ACROSTIC

✏ **Use the letter on each line as the first letter of a way to be responsible.**

R emember to do what I have said I'll do.

E xplain when I have to change my plans.

S _____

P _____

O _____

N otice when someone needs help - and give it!

S _____

I _____

B _____

L _____

E _____

THERE SHOULD BE AN "F" IN RESPONSIBLE.

SO YOU COULD WRITE, "FROGS FREQUENTLY FIX FOOD FOR FATHERS?"

WELL, IT IS A RESPONSIBLE THING TO DO!

THE VALUE OF BEING RESPONSIBLE

God's values are the STANDARD to help me know how to live my life and treat other people

Are you thinking what is in the thought balloon?

HOW CAN YOU KNOW WHAT YOUR VALUES ARE?

Look at the things you DO, SAY, and THINK. If you spend time doing something, then you know it is one of your values.

My name is _____ .

Being responsible _____ important to me.
　　　　　　　　　　is　is not

I _____ spend time thinking about what I've said I'll do,
　　do　do not

and the things I see that need to be done.

Being careful to do what I say I'll do is being responsible.

I can show that being responsible is becoming my

value when I _____ and _____ .

Pretend you are going to write a book about a responsible person that you know.
✎ **On a sheet of paper, design the front of the book jacket for your story.**

WHAT IS BEING MERCIFUL?

BEING MERCIFUL IS . . .
treating someone kindly instead of giving punishment, even when punishment is deserved.

I think being merciful can also mean _____
_____.

God treats us with mercy and wants us to follow His example.

✏️ **Use the code box to find the missing words. Find the number first, and move your finger across the row until your finger is resting in the column under the symbol.**

We are to show mercy to

1♡ 4♡ 3♡ 1👣 1👄 2👄   (FAMILY)

3✋ 4👄 1👣 1✋ 1👁 4✋ 3👁 3👄 2♡   (NEIGHBORS)

1♡ 3👄 1👣 4👄 3✋ 4👣 2♡   (FRIENDS)

4👄 2👣 4👄 3👄 2👄 3👁 3✋ 4👄   (EVERYONE)

	♡	✋	👁	👣	👄
1	F	G	H	I	L
2	S	T	U	V	Y
3	M	N	O	P	R
4	A	B	C	D	E

Being merciful is important to me.
When I treat others in a way they may not deserve, then being merciful becomes one of my values.

Name _____

Date _____

God's values are the STANDARD to help me know how to live my life and treat other people

THE BIBLE TELLS ABOUT BEING MERCIFUL

Abigail Helps David Show Mercy

David and his soldiers were traveling around the country to get away from King Saul, who was trying to kill David. David and his men had to get food from the people who lived in the area and would sometimes help the farmers, as they did by guarding the shepherds and the sheep for Nabal.

1 Samuel 25:2-35

A certain man . . . was very wealthy. . . . His name was Nabal and his wife's name was Abigail. She was an intelligent and beautiful woman, but her husband, a Calebite, was surly and mean in his dealings.

While David . . . sent ten young men and said to them, "Go up to Nabal at Carmel and greet him in my name. Say to him: 'Long life to you . . . to all that is yours!

"'Now I hear that it is sheep-shearing time. When your shepherds were with us, we did not mistreat them, and the whole time they were at Carmel nothing of theirs was missing. Ask your own servants and they will tell you. Therefore be favorable toward my young men, since we come at a festive time. Please give [us] whatever you can find for [us].'"

When David's men arrived, they gave Nabal this message in David's name. Then they waited.

Nabal answered David's servants, "Who is this David? . . . Why should I take my bread and water, and the meat I have slaughtered for my shearers, and give it to men coming from who knows where?"

David's men turned around and went back. When they arrived, they reported every word. David said to his men, "Put on your swords!" So they put on their swords, and David put on his. About four hundred men went up with David, while two hundred stayed with the supplies.

One of the servants told Nabal's wife Abigail: "David sent messengers from the desert to give our master his greetings, but he hurled insults at them. Yet these men were very good to us. . . . see what you can do, because disaster is hanging over our master and his whole household. . . ."

(Read the rest of this story on page 26)

What happened first? ✎ **Write a number by each sentence to put the story in order.** The first one is done for you.

_____ A servant tells Abigail what has happened.
  1   David and his men need food.
_____ Nabal won't give David's men any food.
_____ David thanks Abigail for reminding him to be merciful.

_____ David sends 10 men to ask Nabal for food.
_____ David and his men want to fight Nabal because he won't give them what they earned.
_____ Abigail takes food to David and asks him to show mercy to Nabal.

THE BIBLE TELLS ABOUT BEING MERCIFUL

Abigail Helps David Show Mercy

(1 Samuel 25:2-35 continued from page 25)

Abigail lost no time. She took two hundred loaves of bread, two skins of wine, five dressed sheep, five seahs of roasted grain, a hundred cakes of raisins and two hundred cakes of pressed figs, and loaded them on donkeys. Then she told her servants, "Go on ahead; I'll follow you." But she did not tell her husband Nabal.

As she came riding her donkey . . . , she met them. David had just said, "It's been useless—all my watching over this fellow's property in the desert so that nothing of his was missing. He has paid me back evil for good. . . ."

When Abigail saw David, she quickly got off her donkey and bowed down before David . . . . "My lord, . . . Please let [me] speak to you; . . . pay no attention to that wicked man Nabal. . . .

". . . And let this gift, which [I have] brought to [you], be given to the men who follow you. Please forgive [Nabal's] offense, . . . Let no wrongdoing be found in you as long as you live. Even though someone is pursuing you to take your life, . . ."

David said to Abigail, "Praise be to the LORD, the God of Israel, who has sent you today to meet me. May you be blessed for your good judgment and for keeping me from bloodshed this day and from avenging myself with my own hands. . . ."

Then David accepted from her hand what she had brought him and said, "Go home in peace. I have heard your words and granted your request."

David

Nabal

Abigail

servant

Who said it?

Draw a picture beside each statement to show who said it:

1. _____ "Greet Nabal in my name."

2. _____ "Why should I give my bread and water?"

3. _____ "These men were very good to us. See what you can do."

4. _____ "Nabal is returning evil when I was doing good."

5. _____ "Please forgive Nabal's offense."

6. _____ "God has sent you to me. I grant your request."

PUPPETS FOR A PLAY ABOUT MERCY

✏️ You will need four gloves to use as puppets for the puppet play on pages 29 and 30. First, use the eraser end of a pencil to push a tissue into each glove finger. Then fill the rest of the glove with tissue or wadded paper so the glove can stand alone. Color the puppet pieces and cut out. Glue so each puppet can fit on a glove finger. David and his men (marked with a "D") will use 2 gloves; Nabal and his servants (marked with an "N") —1 glove; and Abigail and her servants (marked with an "A")—1 glove.

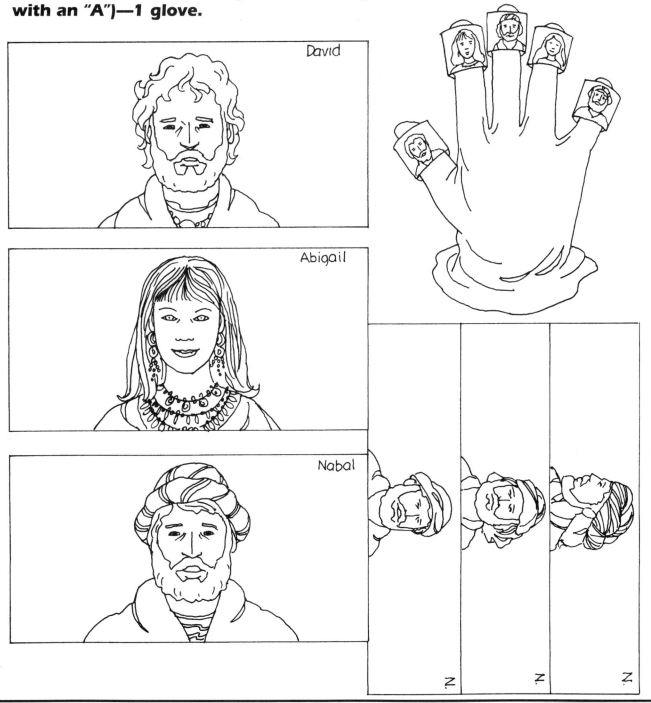

PUPPETS FOR A PLAY ABOUT MERCY

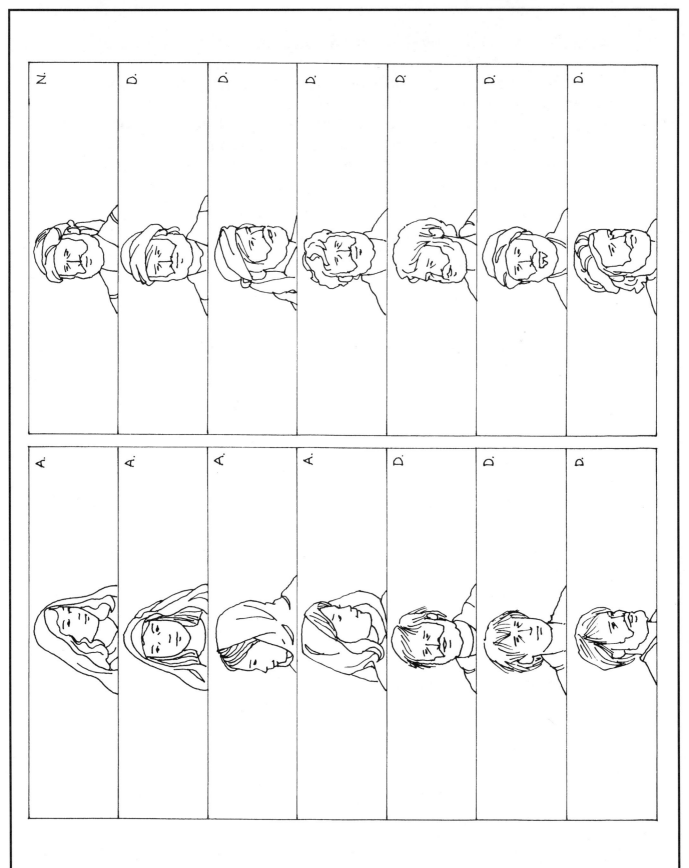

ABIGAIL AND DAVID SHOW MERCY

A Puppet Play based on 1 Samuel 25:2-35

The participants in this exciting true event are: Abigail, David, Nabal, nine of David's men, four of Nabal's servant, and four of Abigail's servants.

PREPARATION: Follow the directions for the puppets on pages 27 and 28. The puppets will be on the glove fingers and moving as a group.

SETTING: This takes place in the country side of Carmel, near Hebron.

[NABAL is sitting among his servants to the far right side as if off in the distance. DAVID and nine of his men enter on the left.]

DAVID: It's time to eat! Are you as hungry as I am? We should ask Nabal if he can give us some food. We've been protecting his sheep and shepherds so he should be glad to help us out. Hey, *(calling and pointing to his men)* Tom, Dan, Levi, Josh, and Cabe. Come over here for a minute. I need you to go to talk to Nabal. This is party time, sheep-shearing time, at his ranch—he'll be in a good mood and share his food with us.

[Five men move in closer to DAVID. One of them speaks.]

DAN: I should think Nabal could share with us. He's the wealthiest farmer around here, with one-thousand goats and three-thousand sheep. That's why he needed our help. He has plenty, of course he'll share.

DAVID: Go to Nabal and tell him that you are bringing greetings.

DAN: I've heard this guy Nabal is mean to everyone who comes by. He may think we are just making all this up.

DAVID: Tell him to ask his own servants about it. They know we were helpful.

DAN: Well, okay, but I hope he doesn't just throw us out of his tent.

DAVID: Ask Nabal to treat us as kindly as we treated his shepherds and sheep. Ask him to give us whatever food he can find.

[DAN and four other men move across the field to where NABAL and his servants are. DAN addresses one of the servants.]

DAN: We bring greetings of good health from David to your master Nabal.

NABAL *(in a mean, grouchy voice)*: What? Who? Who is this David you're talking about? He thinks he's special but I can't be bothered with him—or you! What do you want?

DAN: Good and kind master, we have been kind to your shepherds when they were in the same fields we were. We guarded them and the sheep and nothing was missing or hurt. Now we need food and this is such a festive time for you and your people. Please help us by giving some of your extra food.

ABIGAIL AND DAVID SHOW MERCY

NABAL: Why should I give you my bread, my water, and my meat? Who knows where you come from! Get out of here! Your man David is just a good-for-nothing! I won't give him any food!

[NABAL and his servants leave. The five men go back sadly to DAVID and DAN explains what happened.]

DAN *(forlornly)*: It doesn't look good. Whoever said Nabal is mean is certainly right! Here's exactly what he said *(whispers in David's ear.)*!

DAVID *(shouting)*: What!! Nabal is insulting us. He won't give us food? He doesn't believe that we helped his shepherds? This can't happen! We'll have to get food from him someway. *(looking around the group of men)* Put on your swords. Tell all the others. We'll have two hundred men stay here with our supplies, but tell the other four hundred to come with their swords ready.

[DAVID and the men exit left. ABIGAIL and four servants enter on the right.]

SERVANT: It's trouble, my mistress, I know it's trouble! There were men here from David to talk to our master, but Nabal was mean to them! He yelled at them, and called them names. The men were very respectful.

ABIGAIL: David? He sent men here to talk to Nabal? Do you mean David, the next king?

SERVANT: Oh, please do something, we'll all be killed. Oh, I know we will. You'll do something, won't you?

ABIGAIL: Yes, you might be right. *(talking to herself)* If I went to talk to David and took him food, he might decide to forgive Nabal. It's worth a try. *(to servants)* Come with me. Let's see what we can do.

[ABIGAIL and servants move toward DAVID who is entering from the left with his men.]

DAVID: I can't believe it! We've been protecting Nabal's property and he won't even . . . *(sees ABIGAIL who bows toward him.)*

ABIGAIL: My lord, I would like to speak to you. I want to apologize for Nabal. Please forgive him for what he has said about you. Show him mercy by not fighting back.

DAVID: But he has been very mean to us when we were only kind to him.

ABIGAIL: We've brought food for you. Please accept it as a gift from us. You shouldn't fight with Nabal because he has been mean to you. Show him mercy instead.

DAVID: You are right. Your good plan to show mercy has kept me from sinning against God. We'll accept your gift of food and do as you ask.

[ABIGAIL'S SERVANTS give the food to DAVID's men and ABIGAIL and her party leave.]

DAVID *(to his men)*: God has blessed us today. Let's thank Him for bringing Abigail to talk to us. Then, let's eat!

150-YEAR-OLD CODE

Psalm 103:10
God wants to let us know how He feels about us. He tells us in the Bible about His mercy and love toward us.

 **Use this code called the MORSE Code to figure out the verse.** The dots and dashes are short and long signals for letters. The signals can be written, made by long or short sounds, or sent by flashes of light.

.- = A	-... = B	-.-. = C	-.. = D	. = E
..-. = F	--. = G	.... = H	.. = I	.--- = J
-.- = K	.-.. = L	-- = M	-. = N	--- = O
.--. = P	--.- = Q	.-. = R	... = S	- = T
..- = U	...- = V	.-- = W	-..- = X	
-.-- = Y	--.. = Z			

__ __ __   __ __ ___   __ __ ___   __ __ ___   __ __ __ ___
-.- .- -... / .... .- - .... / -. -. - / -.. . .- .-.. - / .-- .. - ....

__ __   __ __ ___ __   __ __ __ __   __ __ __ ___ __   __ ___
..- ... / .- ..-. - . .-. / --- ..- .-. / ... .. -. ... / -. --- .-.

__ __ __   __ __ __ __ __ __ __ __   __ __   __ __ __ __ __ __ __ ___
.-. . .-- / .- .-. -.. . -.. / ..- ... / .- -.-. -.-. --- .-. -.. .. -. --.

__ __   __ __ __ __   __ __ __ __ __ __ __ __ ____
- --- / --- ..- .-. / .. -. .. --.- ..- .. - .. . ...

Since God does not treat us as we deserve, how can we follow His example in treating others? _____

_____

"INIQUITIES? IS THAT WORD IN OLD CODE TOO?"

"IT MEANS 'SINS,' THE THINGS WE DO WRONG."

MERCIFUL BOOKMARK

✏️ **Make a bookmark to remind yourself that God is merciful and He desires us to be merciful too.**

You need:
- ☐ Two 4 1/2" x 12" pieces of construction paper or felt in contrasting colors
- ☐ Scissors
- ☐ Ruler
- ☐ Glue
- ☐ Marker

✂️ **To make a bookmark:**

1. On one strip of paper or felt, draw a line 4" from one end and another line 4" from the other end.
2. Draw six 4" lines, 1/2" apart, from the top to each 4" line, leaving a 4" x 3 1/2" uncut area in the middle.
3. Weave the 1/2" x 3 1/2" strips through the strips of each end of the long piece of paper or felt, putting the short strips close together.
4. Put a small amount of glue at the ends of each strip so the woven paper or felt will stay in place.
5. Write the words GOD IS MERCIFUL in the middle unwoven section. On the other side, write the words I WILL BE MERCIFUL.

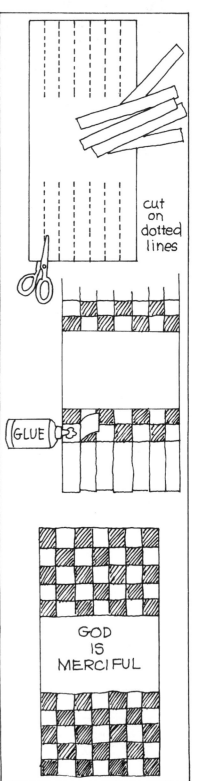

WHAT IS MERCY?

✏️ **Read these difficult situations and then decide what you think each person could do. Write your response in the lines provided.**

What do you do when someone says something bad or untrue about you? Do you tell lies about that person or do you show mercy?

What do you do when someone tells the coach you don't want to play and you lose your position for the upcoming game? You try talking to the coach, but it does no good. Do you do something mean to get even or do you show mercy?

SHOW MERCY TO ALL PEOPLE

God shows mercy to everyone who comes to Him and asks for mercy. He loves <u>everyone</u>! We can follow God's example and show mercy to those around us.

✏️ **Color RED in all the spaces without dots. Color the other spaces BLUE.** What did you find?

When I love and value other people as God does, I can show mercy.

WORDS ABOUT BEING MERCIFUL

These words are lost in this box. ✏️ **Find them by looking across, down, backward, forward, and diagonally. Circle the letters of each word as you find it.**

forgiving   understanding   giving   smiles   kindness   polite
love   sharing   hugs   cooperate   caring   helping

✏️ **Write two of the words about being merciful here.**

_____   _____

What can you do today to show mercy? _____

_____

_____

DOES NOT HITTING ON MY BROTHER COUNT AS BEING MERCIFUL?

SURE! ESPECIALLY SINCE I'M THAT BROTHER!

35

THE BIBLE TELLS ABOUT BEING MERCIFUL

Jesus Tells a Story

Jesus told Peter a story.

Matthew 18:21-35
   Then Peter came to Jesus and asked, "Lord, how many times shall I forgive my brother when he sins against me? Up to seven times?" Jesus answered, "I tell you, not seven times, but seventy-seven times.
   "Therefore, the kingdom of heaven is like a king who wanted to settle accounts with his servants. As he began the settlement, a man who owed him ten thousand talents was brought to him. Since he was not able to pay, the master ordered that he and his wife and his children and all that he had be sold to repay the debt.
   "The servant fell on his knees before him. 'Be patient with me,' he begged, 'and I will pay back everything.' The servant's master took pity on him, canceled the debt and let him go.
   (Read the rest of the story on page 37)

"SETTLE ACCOUNTS" MEANS TO MAKE EVERYTHING EVEN AND UP TO DATE.

Forgiving is like being merciful because _____
_____

Jesus said to forgive someone seventy-seven times (even more times than you think you need to).

How many times would Jesus want you to show mercy? _____

✏️ **Draw lines to finish each sentence.**

In the story Jesus told,

1. The king is like   us.

2. The servants are like   not very much money.

3. Ten thousand talents is worth   God the Father.

4. One hundred denarii is worth   our sin.

5. The debt is an example of   about three million dollars.

THE BIBLE TELLS ABOUT BEING MERCIFUL

Jesus Tells a Story

Jesus told Peter this story.

(Matthew 18:21-35 continued from page 36)
"But when that servant went out, he found one of his fellow servants who owed him a hundred denarii. He grabbed him and began to choke him. 'Pay back what you owe me!' he demanded.

"His fellow servant fell to his knees and begged him, 'Be patient with me, and I will pay you back.'

"But he refused. Instead, he went off and had the man thrown into prison until he could pay the debt. When the other servants saw what had happened, they were greatly distressed and went and told their master everything that had happened.

"Then the master called the servant in. 'You wicked servant,' he said, 'I canceled all that debt of yours because you begged me to. Shouldn't you have had mercy on your fellow servant just as I had on you?' In anger his master turned him over to the jailers to be tortured, until he should pay back all he owed.

"This is how my heavenly Father will treat each of you unless you forgive your brother from your heart."

"DEBT" IS SOMETHING LIKE MONEY THAT IS OWED TO ANOTHER PERSON.

TRUE or FALSE? **If the statement is true, color all the "T" squares. If the statement is false, color all the "F" squares. Write the letters you see in the boxes on the lines below.**

1. The king showed mercy when he canceled a large debt.

2. The king didn't care how the servants treated each other.

3. The first servant received mercy, but did not give it.

4. The king expected the servants to be merciful to each other.

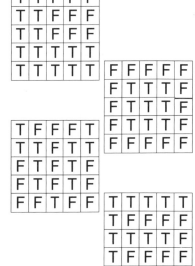

____ ____ ____ ____

A GAME ABOUT MERCY

Play this game to help you think about mercy. You can play by yourself or take turns with a friend.

You need:
- ☐ Poster board
- ☐ Index cards
- ☐ Scissors
- ☐ Markers and crayons

✂ To get ready for the game:
1. Follow the instructions on page 39 for making the large game piece.
2. Find several marbles to roll through the game holes.
3. Make game cards from blank index cards. On each card write one situation that either shows mercy or does not show mercy. Then shuffle the cards. Place half of the cards behind each opening in the game board.

✂ To play:
1. Set up game board.
2. Put a line with string or masking tape at least 24 inches from the game board.
3. Each person, in turn, rolls a marble through one of the two openings. If the marble does not go through an opening, the turn is over and no points are gained or lost.
4. If a marble does go through an opening, then that player picks up a card from the stack where his/her marble went through. The card is read out loud. If the person on the card showed mercy, 100 points are scored. If the person on the card did not show mercy, then 100 points are subtracted.
5. Continue playing until all the cards are used.
6. Add up your score. Keep track of how high it is to see if you can get a higher score next time or try moving the game board further away from the starting line.

A GAME ABOUT MERCY

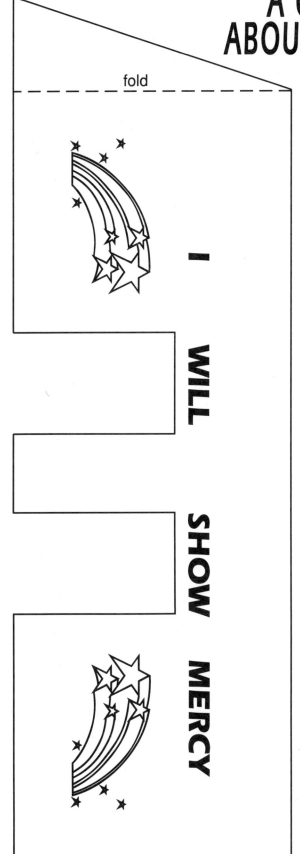

I WILL SHOW MERCY

✂ **To make the game board:**
1. Glue this game piece to poster board and cut it out.
2. Decorate with crayons or markers.
3. Tape two coins or small stones behind each end piece to keep the background standing upright.

LOVING MERCY - MICAH 6:8

✎ **Draw a line to match the meaning with the word. Then write the word on the lines with that number. Finish the statements.**

1. expect, demand   mercy

2. fairly, honestly   humbly

3. not giving punishment   require
   as deserved

4. not proud   justly

Micah 6:8

"And what does the LORD _____ of you?
                              1

To act _____ and to love _____ and
           2   3

to walk _____ with your God."
              4

═══

I am acting _____ when I
                2

_____.

I show that I love _____ when I
                       3

_____.

I show that I am walking _____ with God when I
                              4

_____.

WHERE SHOULD I SHOW MERCY?

✎ **Follow the maze to find your way to Mercy Village.** On the way you will go through places where mercy can be shown everyday.

Jesus told a story about showing mercy as often as needed. Of the places in the maze, which is the easiest place for you to show mercy? _____
the hardest place for you to show mercy? _____

THE VALUE OF BEING MERCIFUL

How can you know what your values are? Look at the things you DO, SAY, and THINK. If you spend time doing something, then you know it is one of your values.

God's values are the STANDARD to help me know how to live my life and treat other people

Are you thinking what is in the thought balloon?

My name is _____.

Being merciful _____ important to me. I _____ spend
                   is   is not   do   do not
time treating others kindly even when they may not deserve it.

I can show that being merciful is becoming my

value when I _____ and _____ .

✎ **On a separate sheet of paper, write a poem about God's mercy and illustrate it.**

VALUE BUILDERS SERIES INDEX
BY VALUE

Accepting
Romans 15:7
Galatians 3:28
Luke 7 — Jesus and the woman with no name
Acts 10 — Peter's vision and visit

Appreciative
See thankful

Attentive
Psalm 34:15
James 1:19
Nehemiah 8 — Ezra reads the law
Luke 10 — Mary listens to Jesus

Caring
See concerned

Choices
See wise

Committed
1 Kings 8:61
Proverbs 16:3
Esther 4 — Esther
John 1 — Andrew follows Jesus

Compassionate
2 Corinthians 1:3-4
1 Peter 3:8
Luke 10 — Good Samaritan
Luke 23 — Jesus on the cross

Concerned
1 Corinthians 12:25
1 John 3:17
Matthew 25 — Jesus teaches to meet needs
Acts 2 — Church provides for each other

Confident
Philippians 4:13
Psalm 139:14
1 Samuel 17 — David and Goliath
Nehemiah 6 — Nehemiah isn't intimidated

Considerate
See respectful, kind

Consistent
1 John 3:18
Psalm 33:4
Matthew 26 — Jesus in the garden
Daniel 6 — Daniel as administrator

Contented
See peaceful

Conviction
Deuteronomy 13:6-8
Acts 4:19-20
Daniel 3 — Blazing furnace and three Hebrews
John 2 — Jesus clears the temple courts

Cooperative
Colossians 3:23-24
Ephesians 4:16
Acts 6 — Disciples share responsibilities
Exodus 18 — Jethro gives Moses a plan

Courageous
Joshua 1:9
Isaiah 41:10
Acts 23 — Paul's nephew
Esther 4 — Esther

Creative
See resourceful

Decision Making
See purposeful

Dedicated
See committed

Dependable
See responsible

Diligent
See persevering, purposeful, responsible

Discerning
See wise

Discipleship
See teachable, prayerful, worshipful, faith, holy

Discipline
See self-disciplined

Empathy
Galatians 6:2
Hebrews 13:3
John 11 — Jesus at Lazarus's death
1 Samuel 19 — Jonathan speaks up for David

Endurance
See persevering, self-disciplined, purposeful

Enthusiasm
See joyful

Fairness
Leviticus 19:15
Romans 12:17
James 2 — Favoritism at a meeting
Matthew 20 — Parable of workers

Faith
John 3:16
Hebrews 11:6
Acts 16 — Philippian jailer
Matthew 8 — Centurion sends servant to Jesus

Faithful
See loyal

VALUE BUILDERS SERIES INDEX
BY VALUE

Fellowship
See friendly

Flexibility
See cooperative, initiative, resourceful

Forgiving
Ephesians 4:32
Leviticus 19:18
Matthew 18 — Parable of unforgiving servant
Genesis 45 — Joseph forgives brothers

Friendly
Luke 6:31
Proverbs 17:17
1 Samuel 18 — David and Jonathan
Acts 9 — Paul and Barnabas

Generosity
Matthew 5:42
Hebrews 13:16
Ruth 2 — Boaz gives grain to Ruth
2 Corinthians 8 — Paul's letter about sharing

Gentle
Matthew 11:29-30
Philippians 4:5
Mark 10 — Jesus and the children
John 19 — Joseph of Arimathea prepares Jesus' body

Genuineness
See sincerity

Giving
See generosity

Goodness
See consistent, holy

Helpfulness
Acts 20:35
Ephesians 6:7-8
Exodus 2 — Miriam and baby Moses
Mark 14 — Disciples prepare Last Supper

Holy
Romans 12:2
Psalm 51:10
Acts 10 — Cornelius
Exodus 3 — Moses and the burning bush

Honest
Leviticus 19:11
Ephesians 4:25
Mark 14 — Peter lies about knowing Jesus
1 Samuel 3 — Samuel tells Eli the truth

Honor
See obedient, respectful, reverence

Hopeful
Jeremiah 29:11
Romans 15:13
Acts 1 — Jesus will return/Ascension
Genesis 15 — Abraham looks to the future

Humble
Psalm 25:9
Romans 12:16
Luke 7 — Centurion asks Jesus to heal son
Matthew 3 — John the Baptist and Jesus

Independent
See confident, initiative

Initiative
Joshua 22:5
Ephesians 4:29
John 13 — Jesus washes feet
Nehemiah 2 — Nehemiah asks to go to Jerusalem

Integrity
See consistent, holy, honest

Joyful
1 Thessalonians 5:16
1 Peter 1:8
Luke 2 — Jesus' birth
Acts 12 — Rhoda greets Peter

Justice
See fairness

Kind
1 Thessalonians 5:15
Luke 6:35
2 Samuel 9 — David and Mephibosheth
Acts 28 — Malta islanders and Paul

Knowledge
See teachable

Listening
See attentive

Long suffering
See patience

Loving
John 13:34-35
1 Corinthians 13:4-7
Luke 15 — Prodigal son
John 11 — Mary, Martha, Lazarus and Jesus

Loyal
1 Chronicles 29:18
Romans 12:5
1 Samuel 20 — David and Jonathan
Ruth 1 — Ruth and Naomi

Meek
See gentle, humble

VALUE BUILDERS SERIES INDEX
BY VALUE

Merciful
Psalm 103:10
Micah 6:8
1 Samuel 25 — Abigail helps David show mercy
Matthew 18 — Unmerciful servant

Obedient
See also respectful
1 Samuel 15:22
Ephesians 6:1
1 Samuel 17 — David takes lunch
Acts 9 — Ananias at Saul's conversion

Patience
Psalm 37:7
Ephesians 4:2
Genesis 26 — Isaac opens new wells
Nehemiah 6 — Nehemiah stands firm

Peaceful
John 14:27
Hebrews 13:5-6
Acts 12 — Peter sleeping in prison
Matthew 6 — Jesus teaches contentment

Peer pressure, response to
See confident, conviction, wise

Persevering
Galatians 6:9
James 1:2-3
Acts 27 — Paul in shipwreck
Exodus 5 — Moses doesn't give up

Praise
See prayerful, thankful, worshipful

Prayerful
Philippians 4:6
James 5:16
Luke 11 — Jesus teaches disciples
Daniel 6 — Daniel prays daily

Pure
See holy

Purposeful
James 1:22
1 Corinthians 15:58
Matthew 26 — Jesus in Gethsemane
Joshua 24 — Joshua serves God

Reliable
See responsible

Repentant
Acts 26:20
1 John 1:9
Luke 15 — Prodigal son
Luke 22 — Peter's denial

Resourceful
Philippians 4:9
1 Peter 4:10
Luke 5 — Man lowered through roof
Luke 19 — Zacchaeus

Respectful
Deuteronomy 5:16
1 Peter 2:17
1 Samuel 26 — David doesn't kill Saul
Acts 16 — Lydia and other believers

Responsible
Galatians 6:4-5
Proverbs 20:11
Acts 20 — Paul continues his work
Numbers 13 — Caleb follows instructions

Reverence
Daniel 6:26-27
Psalm 78:4, 7
Daniel 3 — Blazing furnace and three Hebrews
Matthew 21 — Triumphal entry

Self controlled
See self-disciplined

Self-disciplined
1 Timothy 4:7-8
2 Timothy 1:7
Daniel 1 — Daniel and king's meat
John 19 — Jesus was mocked

Self-esteem
See confident

Sensitivity
See empathy, compassionate, concerned, kind

Service (servanthood)
See cooperative, generosity, helpful, stewardship

Sharing
See generosity, stewardship

Sincerity
Romans 12:9
Job 33:3
Mark 5 — Jairus and his daughter
2 Timothy 1 — Timothy

Stewardship
Luke 3:11
Ephesians 5:15-16
2 Chronicles 31 — Temple contributions
Acts 4 — Believers share

Submission
See humble, respectful, self-disciplined

Supportive
See friendly, loving

VALUE BUILDERS SERIES INDEX
BY VALUE

Sympathy
See compassionate, concerned

Teachable
Joshua 1:8
Psalm 32:8
Luke 2 — Young Jesus in the temple
Acts 18 — Apollos with Priscilla and Aquilla

Thankful
Psalm 28:17
Colossians 3:17
1 Chronicles 29 — Celebrating the temple
Romans 16 — Paul thanks Phoebe, Priscilla and Aquilla

Tolerant
See accepting

Trusting
Proverbs 3:5-6
Psalm 9:10
Acts 27 — Sailors with Paul in shipwreck
2 Kings 18 — Hezekiah trusts God

Trustworthiness
See honest, responsible

Truthful
See honest

Unselfish
Romans 15:1-3
Philippians 2:4
Luke 23 — God gives His Son
John 6 — Boy gives lunch

Wise
Proverbs 8:10
James 3:13
1 Kings 3 — Solomon asks for wisdom
Daniel 1 — Daniel and king's meat

Worshipful
Psalm 86:12
Psalm 122:1
Nehemiah 8 — Ezra and the people worship
Acts 16 — Paul and Silas in jail

VALUE BUILDERS SERIES INDEX
BY SCRIPTURE

Scripture	Story	Value
Genesis 15	Abraham looks to future	Hopeful
Genesis 26	Isaac opens new wells	Patience
Genesis 45	Joseph forgives brothers	Forgiving
Exodus 2	Miriam and baby Moses	Helpful
Exodus 3	Moses and the burning bush	Holy
Exodus 5	Moses doesn't give up	Persevering
Exodus 18	Jethro gives Moses a plan	Cooperative
Leviticus 19:11		Honest
Leviticus 19:15		Fairness
Leviticus 19:18		Forgiving
Numbers 13	Caleb follows instructions	Responsible
Deuteronomy 5:16		Respectful
Deuteronomy 13:6-8		Conviction
Joshua 1:8		Teachable
Joshua 1:9		Courageous
Joshua 22:5		Initiative
Joshua 24	Joshua serves God	Purposeful
Ruth 1	Ruth and Naomi	Loyal
Ruth 2	Boaz gives grain to Ruth	Generosity
1 Samuel 3	Samuel tells Eli the truth	Honest
1 Samuel 15:22		Obedient
1 Samuel 17	David and Goliath	Confident
1 Samuel 17	David takes lunch	Obedient
1 Samuel 18	David and Jonathan	Friendly
1 Samuel 19	Jonathan speaks up for David	Empathy
1 Samuel 20	David and Jonathan	Loyal
1 Samuel 25	Abigail helps David show mercy	Merciful
1 Samuel 26	David doesn't kill Saul	Respectful
2 Samuel 9	David and Mephibosheth	Kind
1 Kings 3	Solomon asks for wisdom	Wise
1 Kings 8:61		Committed
2 Kings 18	Hezekiah trusts God	Trusting
1 Chronicles 29	Celebrating the temple	Thankful
1 Chronicles 29:18		Loyal
2 Chronicles 31	Temple contributions	Stewardship
Nehemiah 2	Nehemiah asks to go to Jerusalem	Initiative
Nehemiah 6	Nehemiah isn't intimidated	Confident
Nehemiah 6	Nehemiah stands firm	Patience
Nehemiah 8	Ezra and the people worship	Worshipful
Nehemiah 8	Ezra reads the law	Attentive
Esther 4	Esther	Committed
Esther 4	Esther	Courageous
Job 33:3		Sincerity
Psalm 9:10		Trusting
Psalm 25:9		Humble
Psalm 28:17		Thankful
Psalm 32:8		Teachable
Psalm 33:4		Consistent
Psalm 34:15		Attentive
Psalm 37:7		Patience
Psalm 51:10		Holy
Psalm 78:4, 7		Reverence
Psalm 86:12		Worshipful
Psalm 103:10		Merciful
Psalm 122:1		Worshipful
Psalm 139:14		Confident
Proverbs 3:5-6		Trusting
Proverbs 8:10		Wise
Proverbs 16:3		Committed
Proverbs 17:17		Friendly
Proverbs 20:11		Responsible
Isaiah 41:10		Courageous
Jeremiah 29:11		Hopeful
Daniel 1	Daniel and king's meat	Self-disciplined
Daniel 1	Daniel and king's meat	Wise
Daniel 3	Blazing furnace and three Hebrews	Conviction
Daniel 3	Blazing furnace and three Hebrews	Reverence
Daniel 6	Daniel as administrator	Consistent
Daniel 6	Daniel prays daily	Prayerful
Daniel 6:26-27		Reverence
Micah 6:8		Merciful
Matthew 3	John the Baptist and Jesus	Humble
Matthew 5:42		Generosity
Matthew 6	Jesus teaches contentment	Peaceful
Matthew 8	Centurion sends servant to Jesus	Faith
Matthew 11:29-30		Gentle
Matthew 18	Unmerciful servant	Merciful
Matthew 18	Parable of unforgiving servant	Forgiving
Matthew 20	Parable of workers	Fairness
Matthew 21	Triumphal entry	Reverence
Matthew 25	Jesus teaches to meet needs	Concerned
Matthew 26	Jesus in Gethsemane	Purposeful
Matthew 26	Jesus in the garden	Consistent
Mark 5	Jairus and his daughter	Sincerity
Mark 10	Jesus and the children	Gentle
Mark 14	Disciples prepare Last Supper	Helpful
Mark 14	Peter lies about knowing Jesus	Honest
Luke 2	Jesus' birth	Joyful
Luke 2	Young Jesus in the temple	Teachable
Luke 3:11		Stewardship
Luke 5	Man lowered through roof	Resourceful
Luke 6:31		Friendly
Luke 6:35		Kind

VALUE BUILDERS SERIES INDEX
BY SCRIPTURE

Reference	Topic	Value
Luke 7	Centurion asks Jesus to heal son	Humble
Luke 7	Jesus and woman with no name	Accepting
Luke 10	Good Samaritan	Compassionate
Luke 10	Mary listens to Jesus	Attentive
Luke 11	Jesus teaches disciples	Prayerful
Luke 15	Prodigal son	Loving
Luke 15	Prodigal son	Repentant
Luke 19	Zacchaeus	Resourceful
Luke 22	Peter's denial	Repentant
Luke 23	God gives His Son	Unselfish
Luke 23	Jesus on the cross	Compassionate
John 1	Andrew follows Jesus	Committed
John 2	Jesus clears the temple courts	Conviction
John 3:16		Faith
John 6	Boy gives lunch	Unselfish
John 11	Jesus at Lazarus's death	Empathy
John 11	Mary, Martha, Lazarus, and Jesus	Loving
John 13	Jesus washes feet	Initiative
John 13:34-35		Loving
John 14:27		Peaceful
John 19	Jesus was mocked	Self-disciplined
John 19	Joseph of Arimathea prepares Jesus' body	Gentle
Acts 1	Jesus will return/Ascension	Hopeful
Acts 2	Church provides for each other	Concerned
Acts 4	Believers share	Stewardship
Acts 4:19-20		Conviction
Acts 6	Disciples share responsibilities	Cooperative
Acts 9	Ananias at Saul's conversion	Obedient
Acts 9	Paul and Barnabas	Friendly
Acts 10	Cornelius	Holy
Acts 10	Peter's vision and visit	Accepting
Acts 12	Peter sleeping in prison	Peaceful
Acts 12	Rhoda greets Peter	Joyful
Acts 16	Paul and Silas in jail	Worshipful
Acts 16	Philippian jailer	Faith
Acts 16	Lydia and other believers	Respectful
Acts 18	Apollos with Priscilla and Aquila	Teachable
Acts 20	Paul continues his work	Responsible
Acts 20:35		Helpful
Acts 23	Paul's nephew	Courageous
Acts 26:20		Repentant
Acts 27	Paul in a shipwreck	Persevering
Acts 27	Sailors with Paul in shipwreck	Trusting
Acts 28	Malta islanders with Paul	Kind
Romans 12:2		Holy
Romans 12:5		Loyal
Romans 12:9		Sincerity
Romans 12:16		Humble
Romans 12:17		Fairness
Romans 15:1-3		Unselfish
Romans 15:7		Accepting
Romans 15:13		Hopeful
Romans 16	Paul thanks Phoebe, Priscilla, and Aquila	Thankful
1 Corinthians 12:25		Concerned
1 Corinthians 13:4-7		Loving
1 Corinthians 15:58		Purposeful
2 Corinthians 1:3-4		Compassionate
2 Corinthians 8	Paul's letter about sharing	Generosity
Galatians 3:28		Accepting
Galatians 6:2		Empathy
Galatians 6:4-5		Responsible
Galatians 6:9		Persevering
Ephesians 4:2		Patience
Ephesians 4:16		Cooperative
Ephesians 4:25		Honest
Ephesians 4:29		Initiative
Ephesians 4:32		Forgiving
Ephesians 5:15-16		Stewardship
Ephesians 6:1		Obedient
Ephesians 6:7-8		Helpful
Philippians 2:4		Unselfish
Philippians 4:5		Gentle
Philippians 4:6		Prayerful
Philippians 4:9		Resourceful
Philippians 4:13		Confident
Colossians 3:17		Thankful
Colossians 3:23-24		Cooperative
1 Thessalonians 5:15		Kind
1 Thessalonians 5:16		Joyful
1 Timothy 4:7-8		Self-disciplined
2 Timothy 1	Timothy	Sincerity
2 Timothy 1:7		Self-disciplined
Hebrews 11:6		Faith
Hebrews 13:3		Empathy
Hebrews 13:5-6		Peaceful
Hebrews 13:16		Generosity
James 1:2-3		Persevering
James 1:19		Attentive
James 1:22		Purposeful
James 2	Favoritism at a meeting	Fairness
James 3:13		Wise
James 5:16		Prayerful
1 Peter 1:8		Joyful
1 Peter 2:17		Respectful
1 Peter 3:8		Compassionate
1 Peter 4:10		Resourceful
1 John 1:9		Repentant
1 John 3:17		Concerned
1 John 3:18		Consistent